APPLE WAT

2021 BEGINNERS GUIDE

A Comprehensive User Manual On How To
Use And Master The Apple Watch 7,
Complete With Tips Tricks And WatchOS 8
Hacks

By

Natasha Waku

Table of content

INTRODUCTION

If you just got the latest apple watch series seven, then you are certainly in for a treat. The new apple watch series boasts many features, and it's the perfect gadget for fitness tracking, on-the-go calling, and messaging.

With the world moving to expand the usability of various everyday gadgets, it's no surprise that the Apple watch series seven is breaking boundaries in traditional watch use. I think it's safe to conclude you get your money's worth in terms of cost and use.

The author of this book, an avid tech lover, has identified that many users of the apple watch series 7 are not fully conversant with using the gadget. Many users are yet to fully grasp the various features of the smartwatch and how to operate them. So going above the standard manual that comes with this smart Watch, this book will dedicate its words to breaking down how you can operate the apple watch series 7.

This book will explore everything about the new app watch series.

You can trust the information you get within these pages, because it is written by a tech researcher, expert, and enthusiast. The author will explore topics like what's new on the smartwatch, basic features, and how to get started.

The book talks about points like setting your watch up for yourself or a relative, connecting the apple watch to a network, apps and apps setting, the fitness app and watch faces, and much more.

In summary, this is a complete and detailed guide on using an apple watch series 7. It is made not just for new users but even for more advanced users who are unsure how to operate certain devices.

Now that we've covered all these, let's move on to the guide.

CHAPTER ONE

What's New on WatchiOS 8?

The newly released apple watch version, iOS 8, released on the 20th of September 2021, has the most advanced and clear display among its predecessors. There are many first time features fitted into this product, making it a must-have. The latest Apple Watch version can be installed by Series 3 and later users. Users of iOS15 can also upgrade to this new version.

The new version comes with more workout messaging, health, display, and app options. The new model is realsed with a unique new portrait watch face feature. Users can now customize their watch face using portrait images from their iPhones.

Rather than a static image display, the portrait image setting uses segmentation data to put apart the background details from the foreground image. This means details like time, battery level, heart rate, and such will appear on the background above the image. And when you fidget with the digital crown, the image pops in and out.

As part of the new features, you get to see world time options for all 24 timezones. There is also a major improvement to the app Wallet which allows for more digital keys. Including an Ultra Wideband for digital car keys.

It also comes with two added workout types open for selection; Pilates and Tai Chi. Then comes a redesigned Home app allowing for easier access to the HomeKit Accessories. You also get to see apps like the Find Items allowing you to locate lost devices and watch weather notifying you of major weather changes.

Finally, you get to see AssistiveTouch to detect hand gesture controls, the Focus feature to ensure maximum attention on each task at hand, the multiple timer feature, and the Always-On-Display setting for several apps.

Customize and share your Watch face
To customize your watch;

1. Press down the digital crown.

2. Press and hold the display

3. Click the edit button.

4. Select features by swiping left and right. To the left, you find edits for complications.

5. Tap your preference, and with the Digital Crown modify it.

6. Once done with your selection, press down the Digital Crown to save the new change.

7. Click the watch face to set it as the present face.

To share your present active watch face;

1. Press down the watch face select share

2. Select or add a contact

3. Add a message using the create message if you choose

4. Send.

Track your sleep in a smarter way

That new iOS8 used by the Apple Watch Series 7 allows you to monitor your sleep. To do so, ensure you have an over 30% charge and have it worn while you sleep. But first, head over to the sleep app to set a sleep schedule or schedules for weekdays, weekends, or more.

The schedule setup has several promptings that can easily be followed. Follow the direction to set a sleep goal, that is, how many hours you wish to sleep, bedtime, wakeup alarm, and timing for sleep mode; this automatically sets up the Do Not Disturb setting. You can modify all these in the future by simply clicking the full schedule tab on the sleep app.

Modify sleep options settings by going to the sleep app.

1. Select sleep focus

2. Adjust settings like

   - Turn On at Wind Down which sets a countdown to your bedtime

   - Sleep Screen; which simplifies the Apple Watch Display minutes before bed

   - Show Time which simply shows the time and date on your watch while on sleep mode

View your sleep history over two weeks from the sleep app.

Countdown to hand washing

The apple watch will detect and count your hand washing time as recommended by WHO. To set it up

1. Head to settings

2. Select Handwashing

3. Activate the handwashing timer

Once the Apple Watch detects handwashing, a 20 seconds timer will begin. It will prompt you to keep washing if you stop before the time. You may set a reminder to remind you at intervals to clean your hands.

1. Go back to the settings app and the Handwashing section

2. Click on a reminder and set an appropriate time or times

Manage a family member's Watch

For a relative who has the Apple watch but not an iPhone, you can manage their apple watch for them. To do so, you must be the family organizer of the family sharing group.

To manage the watch, your iPhone must be with Bluetooth range, 10 meters or 33 feet from the apple watch. To modify settings like General, Cellular, Accessibility, Emergency SOS, Schooltime, Screentime, Activity, App Store, Handwashing, and more,

1. Launch the apple watch app using your iPhone

2. Select all watches

3. Select family watches

4. Select the watch to be managed

5. Click done.

Smartly manage your home

With the apple home app, you can manage HomeKit accessories like Locks, Smart TVs, Thermostats, and more. Your initial entrance to the app through your iPhone should prompt you to form rooms, include HomeKit enabled devices and accessories, and set up scenes. These accessories and rooms will be open for control through the watch.

To view your home status;

1. Click on Home on your watch

2. Select one accessory or room you wish to check

For multiple homes,

- Launch the Home

- Tap a home from the Home Screen

- If one Home Screen is already up, click your back or return button

- Select another home.

Unlock iPhone with Apple watch

Unlock your iPhone using your Apple watch.

1. Go to your iPhone setting and select Face ID & Passcode.

2. Add your passcode

3. Activate Apple watch

If you want to unlock an iPhone with a face mask on, have the watch on your wrist

1. Wake up your iPhone

2. Look at the screen

3. You should receive a tap from your watch to indicate your iPhone has been unlocked.

New Watch faces

There are several new faces on the Apple Watch Series 7. They are all customizable but note that not all faces are available to all regions. They include;

1. Contour

2. Modular Duo

Apple Watch 6 and 7 compared

There are notable differences between the Apple Watch 6 and 7 series. If you look forward to getting either of these two watches, here are some notable differences.

	Apple Watch 7	Apple Watch 6
Sizes	41mm, 45mm	40mm, 44mm
Colors	Aluminum: Blue, Green, Midnight	Aluminium: Blue, Gold,
	Product(RED), Starlight Stainless steel:	Product (RED), Silver,
	Gold, Graphite, Silver, Titanium:	Space Gray Stainless Steel:

	Space Black (DLC), Silver.	Gold, Graphite. Sliver Titanium:
		Space Black (DLC), Silver
Durability	50m water resistance	50m water resistance
	IP6X dust resistance	
	50 percent thicker front crystal	
Battery	Up to 18 hours USB-C	Up to 18 hours USA-A

	Magnetic fast charging cable	magnetic charging cable

CHAPTER TWO

Set up and get started

You must take a few steps to properly configure and begin using the Apple Watch Series 7.

Get Started

Setting up your Apple Watch Series 7 requires an iPhone that runs on the latest iOS version.

Choose a watch face

1. Swipe right or left from edge to edge on your Watch

2. Stop when you get to your desired watch face to use

Select an app

The Apple Watch contains different apps such as health, fitness, time, keeping tasks, and more. You can decide from these apps fitting your demand.

1. Go to the home page

2. Scroll through the various apps

3. Click to select one

About your Apple Watch

It is a smartwatch filled with features useful to various activities from health, lifestyle to tracking, monitoring, and control.

How to set up and pair your Apple Watch with iPhone

First, turn on the Bluetooth on your iPhone and make sure you are connected to either a cell network or Wi-Fi.

1. Switch on your Apple Watch
2. Maintain closer distance between your Apple Watch and iPhone
3. Place iPhone over the animation
4. Set as new or backup restore

Apple Watch Gestures

The AssistiveTouch allows the use of hand gestures for navigating and using the Apple Watch. Here's a simple way to turn it on

1. Launch Settings on the Watch
2. Go to Accessibility
3. Tap AssistiveTouch
4. Turn it on and confirm

5. Alternatively, tap the "Try it out" to see a visual display of it

Now that you have activated the AssistiveTouch, here are some default actions to navigate using hand gestures

1. Pinch: moves you to the next item
2. Double pinch: move back an item
3. Clench: Tap an item
4. Double clench: bring back the action menu

Unpair your Apple Watch from iPhone

To unpair your Watch from your iPhone, follow these simple steps

1. Ensure your iPhone and Watch are not far from each other to unpair
2. Using your iPhone, launch the Apple Watch app
3. Navigate to the "My watch Tab" and tap all watches

4. You will find a button close the list of watch, then unpair. Tap on the button

5. Unpair Apple Watch by tapping "unpair."

The Apple Watch App

Most later iPhone versions will have the app preinstalled, but if you do not have it, then

1. Go to your app store

2. Search for watch

3. Hit download

4. You should see the watch icon on your app list.

How to charge Apple Watch

1. Get an Apple watch charger and complete setup.

2. Place the charger on a flat surface

3. Connect your charging cable to the power adapter (It is sold separately)

4. Connect your adapter into a power source

Note that the fast charging feature may not support every region

How to put your Apple Watch in power-saving mode

At 10% battery life, your Watch will automatically alert you. It will ask if you need to switch to a power reserve. To put it on power-saving,

1. Swipe from up the face to access the control center
2. Turn on power-saving mode
3. Tap the battery percentage
4. Drag or move the slider of the power saver
5. Tap proceed

Alter language and dimensions of the Apple Watch

For altering the language or region of an Apple Watch;

1. Tap on the Apple Watch app on your iPhone
2. Click on my match and navigate to General
3. Navigate to language and region
4. Click on custom
5. Tap watch language

Setting the dimensions of the Apple Watch

1. Tap and open the Settings on your Apple watch
2. Scroll to general
3. Select orientation and change to left or right

To remove and change the Apple bands. Follow these steps

1. Carefully press the button for the band release on the Watch
2. Carefully slot in the band across for its removal
3. Slot in a new band gently

Do not slide in the band forcefully. If you encounter issues during the removal or fixing process, press the band release button once more time.

Fastening your Apple Watchband

These devices are designed to fit perfectly, on the wrist and the hand. To fit well on the hand, the Apple Watch back requires skin contact such as detection of the wrist, haptic notifications, and heart rate sensor. The proper wearing of the Watch allows skin breathing which helps the sensor work effectively.

How to stay healthy with your Apple Watch?

Among the varieties of features to enjoy on the Watch is how to monitor your health.

1. View health information. This is possible by entering a few health details of yours via the health app. The information you entered can be seen on your Watch

2. Heart rate monitoring

3. Taking an electrocardiogram (ECG) for checking the rhythm of your heat

4. Hearing protection

5. Menstural cycle tracking

6. Fall detection

7. Sleep tracking

8. Hand washing for twenty seconds

Pedometer

The Apple Watch pedometer is an app designed as ActivityTracker. It is designed for monitoring everyday tasks. The pedometer uses the motion processor to provide important statistics about any physical engagement in a day. Some of these activities include the step you take, covered distance, and the calories burnt.

Fitness App

The fitness app on the Watch is designed for keeping track of daily movement throughout the day. The App is also designed to encourage and help you meet fitness goals. It also helps track how you stand, move, and minutes spent working out or exercising.

How to get important health information with Apple Watch 7

You can get important details with Apple Watch 7 by adding health details and medical ID. You could follow these tips if you forgot to include your family member's health details while setting up your health information

1. Launch the Apple Watch app on your iPhone

2. Click all watches

3. Select and click the watch via family watches

4. Click done

5. Click health and do any of these

- To edit or enter information such as weight, date of birth, or height, tap health details
- Clicking on Medical ID lets you to include emergency contacts and more

Sleep and diet

The app helps to meet sleep and diet goals. If you put on this device to bed, it will help in tracking your sleep. You can know about how you have slept by opening the sleep app. It will show you your sleep and diet analysis over the past few weeks.

Heart health notifications

The heart rate allows users to enable notifications from the heart rate app on the Watch. This alerts them whenever they have either irregular heart rhythms, low or high heartbeats.

Menstrual cycle tracking

The health app on your iPhone helps in tracking your menstrual cycle in the Apple Watch. If you switch on the notifications, it tells when you should have your period next or near your fertile window.

Track fitness, exercise, and recovery status

You can keep track of your fitness, exercise, and recovery status on your Apple Watch. Access these features under the heart rate app on your Watch.

Thorough hand washing

This reminds you when next to clean your hands. The Apple Watch also detects how often your hands are washed by sending haptic feedback to the wrist. You will notice a display of soap bubbles on your Watch face during the wash process. A thumbs-up will pop up after 20 seconds.

How to interact with Apple Watch

There are many ways to interact with the Apple Watch. You can message, check on your health and diet for the day, take pictures and get various notifications. To do this

1. Turn the Watch on

2. Open the Home screen

3. Explore any of the apps available by tapping them

Send Message

1. Open the messaging app

2. Navigate to the top of the screen

3. Tap "new message."

4. Tap add contact

5. Search a contact or input a number

6. Tap create message

Get notifications

This allows you to customize and adjust how and when you can be notified of events on your Apple Watch.

1. Head to the Watch app available on iPhone

2. Select the tab My Watch

3. To the top, there wi be a tab Notifications

4. Click it

5. Click the native app

6. A list of app notifications will appear

7. Allow, Deny, or send to Center.

To take a photo on the Watch

1. Launch the camera app
2. Place iPhone to the object and use the Watch as a viewfinder
3. Turn the digital crown to zoom in or out
4. Tap the key area of the shot for exposure adjustment
5. Tap the shutter button to snap

CHAPTER THREE

Set up Apple Watch for a family member

You can set up and managing Apple Watch for an individual without iPhone with this feature. Doing so demands that you are the family organizer or a parent.

How to set up a family member's Apple Watch

1. Switch on the family member's Apple Watch
2. Press, hold until you get a display of the Apple logo
3. Get your phone closer to it and wait until the pairing screen comes up on your iPhone
4. Hit continue
5. Tap "set up family member" and tap continue

6. Place your iPhone in a good position for the Apple Watch to appear in the viewfinder

7. Hit "set up Apple Watch."

8. Complete all instructions to complete set up

How to use Apple Cash Family

1. Launch the Wallet app for managing the Apple Watch

2. Tap the Apple Cash card

3. Tap the three-dotted horizontal lines

4. Swipe up

5. Tap the name under family

6. Choose an option; choose a relative to send money to or get notifications when a family member transact

How to set up Apple cash family with Apple Watch 7

1. Open settings on the family's organizer's iPhone
2. Click on your name
3. Tap family sharing
4. Click on the Apple Cash
5. Select a child or teen
6. Click on set up Apple Cash
7. Follow all popup instructions to complete set up
8. Tap send money
9. Lock your Apple Cash to prevent unwanted transactions

How to get started with SchoolTime

1. Launch the Apple Watch app on your iPhone used for managing your watch
2. Select all watches
3. Hit the watch before family watches

4. Click done and tap schoolTime

5. Turn it on and click on "edit schedule."

6. Select the desired days to be active

7. To add time for various schedules, click on add time

How to play music

1. Launch the Music app

2. Navigate to the screen top

3. Tap Listen now to access a playlists

4. Select a category, playlist, or albums

5. Select play

How to see health and activity reports

1. Once you complete the activity goals, launch the health app on the iPhone

2. Select share

3. Select the name of the family member under sharing with you

4. Select activity
5. Select the timeline to view the activeness of members

Track progress with Apple Health

1. Launch the Activity app on the Watch

2. Locate the three rings

3. The number of calories you burn is indicated by the red move ring

4. A green exercise ring indicates activities completed.

5. The blue stand ring indicate your standing times and movement for a minimum of a minute in each sixty-minutes

Set Up iCloud Reminders

1. Navigate to settings

2. Scroll to "your name iCloud."

3. Turn reminders on

4. Open the reminders app to view a list of reminders stored in the iCloud

Upgrading reminders

Ensure you're connected to the internet to upgrade your reminder if you're launching the app for the first time. To upgrade it, tap the upgrade now to start the process.

CHAPTER FOUR

Here are the basic features and items on the site.

Apps on Apple Watch

They include

- Activity

- Alarms

- App Store

- Audiobooks

- Blood Oxygen (restricted in some regions)

- Calculator

- Calendar

- Camera Remote

- Compass

- Contacts

- Cycle Tracking

- EGG (restricted in some regions)

- Find Device

- Find Items

- Find People

- Heart Rate

- Home

- Mail

- Maps

- Memoji

- Messages

- Mindfulness

- Music

- News (restricted in some regions)

- Noise

- Now Playing

- Phone

- Photos

- Podcasts

- Reminders

- Remote

- Settings

- Shortcuts

- Sleep

- Stocks

- Stopwatch

- Timers

- Tips

- Voice Memos

- Walkie Talkie (restricted in some regions)

- Wallet

- Weather

- Workout

- World Clock.

Status icons
- Charging icon ⚡

- Low battery icon ⚡

- Airplane mode icon ✈

- Do not disturb 🌙

- Theater mode 🎭

- Wi-Fi network 📶

- GPS+Cellular

- Apple Watch not connected to iPhone icon

- Apple Watch with GPS+Cellular has lost connection

- Water Lock icon

- Notification ↪

- App using location services icon ↗

- Locked icon 🔒

- Sleep mode

How to get more apps

1. Launch the App Store on your watch
2. Turn the digital crown for browsing featured apps
3. If you want to see more apps, tap you may choose a category or tap see all
4. By tapping "tap get," you get a free app
5. To buy, tap the price

How to use shortcuts

1. Launch the Shortcuts app on the Watch
2. Tap a shortcut

Add a shortcut

1. Launch the Shortcuts app

2. Tap the three horizontal dotted lines in the top-right corner of a shortcut
3. Tap the three straight horizontal lines on the shortcut screen
4. Turn on "show on Apple Watch."

Control Center

The Watch control center allows easy access to check various things such as a battery, silent mode, focus selection, airplane mode, turn to watch into a flashlight, and lots more.

Switch an app to the Apple Watch

1. Launch the Dock by pressing the side button under the digital crown
2. Swipe up or down to go to the desired app to use
3. Tap the app when you see it

How to open apps

Opening apps on the Apple Watch depends on your view. For grid view, if you are already seeing your apps, tap Open to launch it. By turning the digital crown, you can launch the center displayed app. For list view, turn the digital crown and tap an app to open

Open an app from your Dock

1. Press the side button
2. Turn the digital crown. Alternatively, you may swipe up or down
3. Tap your desired app to launch
4. Push the side button to close the duck

Close an app from the Dock

1. Push the side button on the Watch to bring up the Dock
2. Swipe the screen up or down
3. You can locate the app to close using the digital crown
4. You can close the app with the X icon after swiping the app to the left

How to organize apps

1. Push the digital crown to take you to the home screen
2. Depending on your view, press and hold an app
3. Tap edit apps
4. Drag the app touched to a new spot
5. Push the digital crown when you finish

Move an app to a folder

1. Push the digital crown to take you to the home screen

2. Depending on your view, press and hold an app

3. Move app to your desired folder

Rename an app

iOS does not support app renaming. It is only possible to rename folders. Each app icon provides its app name automatically. It is impossible to rename apps on the springboard.

Delete an app

1. Bring out all apps on the Apple Watch by pressing the digital crown

2. For grid view, press and hold the app to delete until app icons jiggle

3. App icons may not jiggle if you press too hard
4. Hit delete button
5. For list viewing, swipe left on the app to delete
6. Tao the red button to delete
7. Press the digital crown

How to tell time
1. Raise your wrist to tell time
2. Hear the time by opening settings, tapping the clock, and turning on speak the time
3. Hold two fingers on the watch face to hear the time

How to set text size, brightness, sounds, and haptics
To adjust the above, launch the Settings on the watch

- Text size: Tap text size and tap the letters. Alternatively, adjust the text size by turning the digital crown
- Brightness: Adjust the brightness by tapping the brightness controls for adjustment. Or, you may use the digital crown to adjust it

To adjust sound, do the following

- Launch the Settings App on the Watch
- Tap sound and haptics
- Adjust by tapping the digital crown or using the volume control under the alert volume

To adjust haptic

- Launch Settings App on the Watch
- Tap sounds and haptic
- Turn on haptic alerts
- Select either prominent or default

Siri

Siri is a virtual assistant open to all modern version iOS users.

How to launch Siri from your Watch

1. Speak to your Apple Watch by raising your wrist
2. Say "Hey Sir" followed by your command
3. Tap the Siri button on the face of the Apple Watch
4. Press and hold the digital crown until the listening indicator pop up, followed by your command

Set a reminder from Siri

Siri can remind you of important upcoming events on your Apple Watch. Add both home and work addresses to your card. This will help Siri set reminders related to location.

1. Tap edit
2. Add address (work or home)
3. Tap done

Siri Suggestions

Siri is designed to analyze device usage and apps for providing personalized suggestions and quality search results. Each time you use the Siri suggestions, any information you send to Apple has no identification with you. It is connected to a fifteen-minute random, rotating device-generated identifier.

How to see and respond to notifications

1. Raise your wrist once you notice a notification
2. Navigate to the notification bottom by turning the digital crown
3. Tap a button there
4. Swipe down on a notification to clear it

How to create a Medical ID

1. Launch the Health App on your iPhone connected to your Apple Watch
2. Tap the profile picture located at the top right
3. Tap Medical ID
4. Input your details

CHAPTER FIVE

Connecting Apple Watch to network

This is how to connect the Apple Watch to various networks

How to use Apple Watch 7 with a mobile network

1. Launch Apple Watch App on your iPhone
2. Navigate to "My Watch Tab"
3. Tap cellular
4. Tap "set up cellular" and follow each instruction to complete set up
5. In some cases, you may need to contact your carrier

How to connect Apple Watch to a Wi-Fi network

1. Launch the Settings app on the Watch

2. Tap Wi-Fi. (This allows automatic network searching)

3. Select your desired network to join

4. On password request, input scribble or the Apple Watch keyboard

5. Select join

6. Your device should be ready for use

How to wash your hands with Apple Watch 7

Your Apple watch easily detects hand washing immediately you begin, encouraging you to keep washing for 20 seconds as recommended by WHO.

1. Launch the Settings app on the Apple watch

2. Select hand washing

3. Turn on timer

If you don't wash up to the recommended time by WHO, the app will encourage you to continue.

How to move from one device to the other with Apple Watch

Moving from one device to another with a new Apple Watch requires certain steps.

1. Update your old iPhone device
2. Check Activity settings and Health
3. Back up your old iPhone
4. Set up new iPhone
5. Launch the Apple Watch on the new device

How to connect to Bluetooth headphones or speakers

1. Launch the Settings app on the Apple Watch

2. Tap Bluetooth

3. Select the device once it pops up

Monitor your headphone volume

1. Touch and hold the screen bottom of the Apple Watch

2. Swipe up to access the control center

3. Select edit

4. Tap + close to the button or to add it

5. You can open the control center while listening to headphones connected to the Apple Watch

6. You can see the volume level as indicated by a meter

How to unlock iPhone with Apple Watch

1. Raise your Apple Watch on your wrist. However, make sure you don't have a mask, glasses, or any other thing that can cover your face
2. To unlock your iPhone, look at the screen

How to manage fall detection

1. Launch Apple Watch on iPhone
2. Tap my Watch tab
3. Tap Emergency SOS
4. Switch fall detection to on or off

CHAPTER SIX

Apple Watch faces

The apple watch series comes with several watch faces fit for different styles and interests.

Apple Watch faces and features

- Activity Analog: Displays the Activity progress in analog format
- Activity Digital: Display Activity progress digitally
- Artist: A visually engaging face that changes whenever you tap display
- Astronomy: You can see a non-stop update of the Earth in a 3D model
- Breath: The display encourages relaxation and mindful breathing
- California: This watch face shows Roman and Arabic numerals. However, the face is not available to

all iPhone Apple Watch except SE and 4

- Chronograph: Displays measurement of time in actual increments. It also comes with a stopwatch

- Chronograph Pro: By tapping the bezel that surrounds the main twelve-hour Dial, it changes into the chronograph

- Color: The color shows the time and any added feature in your bright color choices

- Contour (only available on the Apple Watch 7): This Watch's face changed to highlight the current color. The numerals are custom designed and fit perfectly on the Watch face

- Count Up: This face is used in tracking elapsed time

- Explorer: This feature green dots that helps to signal the Cellular strength
- Fire and water: Each time you raise your wrist or tap your Watch face, this animation pops up
- GMT: Here, you can see a twelve-hour display clock for the local time and a twenty-four-hour time for tracking the second time zone
- Gradient: Restricted on some Apple Watch, this clock face features gradients with a time movement
- Infograph: Restricted on some Apple Watches, it displays about eight rich, full-color complications, including subsidies
- Infograph Modular: Display about six rich, full-color complications. Not available on all Apple Watches

- Kaleidoscope: Choose a picture for creating a Watch face of various colors and shapes. To change the pattern, turn the digital crown
- Liquid Metal: Animation pop up whenever you tap the display or raise the wrist
- Memoji: Contains every single created Memojis. Restricted on some series except the SE and Series 4 and later
- Meridian: The meridian features fullscreen a classic look with four subdials
- Mickey Mouse and Minnie Mouse: Both characters give you a whimsical time view. Uniquely, they rotate their arms to indicate the time
- Modular: Enjoy a grid layout and digital time display. Additionally,

you may add other features for daily view

- Modular compact: You can select about three complications, including analog or digital Dial. Available on Series 4 and later and SE Watches.

- Modular Duo: (Only available on the Series 7) Display digital time and about three complications. Two of these complications are large. It also features a rectangular option that allows viewing the most important complications.

- Motion: Shows a beautifully designed animated theme

- Numerals: This features the display of time with analog hands above the large hour marker. You can so change it by choosing from various colors and typefaces to combine as you wish

- Numerals Duo: Large numbers font
- Numerals Mono: Large numbers font
- Photos: Each time you tap the display or raise your wrist, a new photo pops up. This Apple Watch face support choosing album, memory, or about twenty-four custom photos
- Portraits: Portrait mode photos for creating multilayered watch face with the depth
- Pride Analog: Feature a rainbow flag inspiration. The color thread moves by turning the digital crown
- Pride Digital: Feature a rainbow flag inspiration. The color thread moves by turning the digital crown
- Pride   Woven: Featurearainbowflaginspiration. The color thread moves by turning the digital crown

- Simple: You can add detail to both Dial and features using this minimalistic and elegant Watch face
- Siri: Display important and timely events
- Solar Dial: (Apple Watch SE and Apple Watch Series 4 and later) Helps to track the sun
- Solar Graph: Display the position of the sun
- Stripes: Choose your favorite stripes number. You can also rotate the angles (Apple Watch SE and Apple Watch Series 4 and later)
- Time-lapse: Display a natural time-lapse video
- Toy Story: Raising your wrists to allow you to see your favorite toy story pop up

- Typograph: Enjoy three custom fonts (Apple Watch SE and Apple Watch Series 4 and later)
- Unity: Pan-African inspired that changes when there is movement (Apple Watch SE and Apple Watch Series 4 and later)
- Utility: See at a glance and ability to add about three complications
- Vapor: Raise your wrist to see animation display
- World Time: Track 24-hour time zone at a time
- X-Large: Enjoy the largest display

Analogous Activity

The Analogous Activity shows the Activity progress on the watch face, superimposed over the traditional analog clock.

Astrophysics

This app allows you to cover the solar system at the snap of your finger.

Breathe

The display encourages relaxation and mindful breathing

Chronograph

Displays measurement of time in actual increments. It also comes with a stopwatch

Water and Fire

Each time you raise your wrist or tap your Watch face, this animation pops up

How to customize the watch face

1. Press digital crown
2. Touch and hold the Watch face
3. Swipe left or right to choose a Watch face
4. Tap edit

5. To select a feature, swipe left or right
6. Turn the digital crown to change it

Change the face

1. To access other watch faces, swipe from one edge to the other edge
2. Touch and hold the watch face to access other available faces.
3. Tap on your favorite when you find it

How to explore the Face Portfolio

To explore available faces

1. Launch the face gallery
2. Choose a feature for a face

Activate the Face Portfolio

1. Go to the Watch face by tapping it
2. Touch and hold the Watch face
3. Swipe right

4. Tap + button
5. Turn the digital crown to select your choice

How to share Apple Watch faces

1. Open Watch app
2. Select the face to share
3. Tap share button
4. Choose your mode of sharing
5. Find the recipient to share the face with
6. Send

CHAPTER SEVEN

Apple Fitness+

The AppleFitness+ is designed to guide users throughout their various workout sessions. Additionally, they offer meditation based on what you do with the workout. They are perfect for people with schedules that find it difficult to engage in workout sessions.

All about Apple Fitness+

The AppleFitness+ helps to track all workouts by offering intelligent recommendations. Users can explore individual workouts or mediations.

How to search Fitness+ exercises

1. Launch the fitness app
2. Tap Fitness+

3. Search for workouts and exercise

Refine and arrange exercise

1. Launch the fitness app
2. Checkout existing workouts or check out a new release
3. Tap on your favorite workout to see details
4. Tap add

How to subscribe to Apple Fitness +

1. Launch the fitness app on your iPhone connected to the Apple Watch
2. Tap Fitness+
3. Tap the free trial button
4. Follow the instructions as required
5. Sign in with your Apple ID for subscription confirmation

Download the Fitness app

1. Go to the App Store
2. Find fitness app
3. Tap Download

How to start a Fitness+ workout

1. Launch the fitness app
2. Tap Fitness+
3. Choose your favorite workout at the screen top
4. Choose a workout from the available categories
5. Follow the instructions that follow

If you do not have the Fitness+ app, you can visit the App Store to download it

How to halt and resume a Fitness+ workout

To pause a workout on the Apple Watch

1. Press both the digital crown and side button at the same time
2. Swipe right
3. Tap pause to halt your workout

To resume workout on the Apple Watch

1. Repeat the same process by tapping both the digital crown and the side button at the same time
2. Tap resume

How to review and stop a Fitness+ exercise

On the Apple Watch

1. Swipe right
2. Tap end
3. View your workout summary on the Watch face immediately you stop
4. To return to workout, tap done

How to change what's on the screen during a Fitness+ exercise

You can change the on-screen metrics during the workout. Here is how to change it

1. While you work out, tap the button that is displayed. Tap the button
2. Turn off all metrics

Note that all metrics are safely collected but not shown on the screen

How to download a Fitness+ exercise

Downloaded workouts allow you to work out even when you are not connected to the cellular network

1. Launch Fitness app
2. Tap Fitness+
3. Download workout

CHAPTER EIGHT

Apps

Learn how to use each app on the Apple Watch Series 7.

How to use the Activity App

1. On the Apple Watch, launch the Activity App
2. Swipe up to see the details for every single ring
3. To see more, swipe up again (these include all the steps you take, the distance you cover, and workouts)
4. Swipe up to all summary

How to use the Alarm App

1. Launch the Alarm App
2. Select the "Add Alarm"
3. Choose AM or PM

4. Tap the minute or hours (This is important if you want to use the 24-hour clock)
5. To adjust, turn the digital crown
6. Tap "done"

How to use the Audiobooks App

1. Launch the Apple Books app
2. At the screen bottom, tab the Audiobooks tab
3. Check out new and featured audiobooks from here
4. Click on the price to purchase any audiobook of your choice

How to use the Blood Oxygen App

You must meet certain requirements to use Blood Oxygen. You will need to the following

1. Check the availability of blood oxygen in your region
2. Update your device
3. Ensure you are above 18

To use Oxygen App

1. Launch Health App
2. Follow the instructions
3. After setting it up, launch the Blood Oxygen App on the Apple Watch to measure blood oxygen levels.

Establish a Blood Oxygen System

1. Launch the Health App on your iPhone

2. Follow the instructions

3. If the steps do not show, browse the tab, tap respiratory, blood, oxygen, and tap enable

4. Measure your old after establishing the Blood Oxygen App

How to use the Calculator App

1. Launch the Calculator App on your Apple Watch

2. Tap numbers

3. Tao operators to get an outcome or result

How to use the Calendar App

1. Launch the Calendar App. Alternatively, you can tap on the date on the displayed calendar on your screen

2. Scroll to see upcoming events by turning the digital crown

3. To see an event, tap to see the details about it

How to use the Camera Remote App

The camera remote app is a tool that allows the watch to function as a remote for taking pictures with the iPhone. With it, you can preview an image before taking the shot and set a shutter timmer.

Take a picture

1. Launch Camera Remote App on the Apple Watch

2. Use Apple Watch as a viewfinder by positioning your iPhone to frame the shot

3. Turn the digital crown to zoom in or out pictures

4. Tapping the key area allows exposure adjustment
5. Tap the shutter button to take pictures

How to use the Compass App

1. Launch the Compass app on your Apple Watch
2. Set bearing by scrolling down
3. Tap bearing
4. Adjust with the digital crown

How to use the Cycle Tracking

1. Launch the Health App
2. Tap browse at the lower right to see the display of health categories
3. Tap cycle tracking
4. Tap get started and follow the instructions
5. Tap turn on

How to use the ECG App

1. Ensure your Apple Watch is snug

2. Launch ECG app on your Watch

3. Place your arms on a flat surface or lap

4. Hold your finger on the digital crown with the hand opposite your watch. However, you should avoid pressing the digital crown during this process

5. Wait for 30 seconds for recording

6. Save any symptom observed by tapping done

How to use the 'Find People' App

1. Launch the "Find People App"

2. Tap your any of your list of friends

3. Return to your friend lists by tapping the back symbol located in the top-left corner

Heart Rate

The Heart Rate app on the Apple Watch allows you to see your current heart rate. You can also see your average walking rate and resting rate. As long as you have this device on you, it will continue to measure your heart rate.

CHAPTER NINE

App Settings

There are many app settings you can use to customize your device better.

How to use the Home App

The home app consisting of all apps and features comes with no settings. The app is preset. To customize what you see on the home app, you will need to customize other features like the watch face and the app setting.

How to use the Maps App

The map app comes with a few settings. Once you open the app and set your destination, you can

Choose alternative routes,

1. Wait for another route to appear

2. Click

Switch to a different transportation mode;

1. public

   - Click the greater than sign

   - Select one of the buses, subway icons

2. private

   - Click the greater than sign

   - Select one of the walking, cycling, transit, driving icons

Take routes with no

1. tolls and highways

- Wait for the driving route to display

- By the side, next to the destination address, click it

- Turn the option on

2. Heavy traffic and hills.

- Wait for the cycling route to display

- By the side, next to the destination address, click it

- Turn the option on

How to use the MemojiApp

You can use the app to create, edit, duplicate or delete a memoji.

3. Open the app on your watch

4. Set it up if you have never used it before; click the get started button

5. Follow the promptings

Once you are all set up, you can try out other features

To edit

- Tap individual features of the memoji.

- Turn the Digital Crown to explore each features variation

To create a watch face with a memoji

- Scroll to the bottom of the memoji app

- Select create a watch face

To duplicate

- Scroll to the bottom of the app

- Select duplicate

To delete

- Scroll to the bottom of the page

- Select delete

Make a Memoji

To make your personalized memoji,

1. Open the app on your watch

2. Click get started and follow the promptings if you have not used the app before.

3. Otherwise, scroll down to your previous creations.

4. Click the add button

5. Select a memoji

6. Click on features of the memoji

7. Use the digital crown to explore variations of each feature Once you are done modifying it, select done

How to use the Messages App

1. Click the message app

2. At the top of the screen, select add a new message

3. Select the contact

4. Create your message

5. Set the language if applicable

6. Send.

You can compose a message on the app either through an on-screen keyboard, scribble with your finger, audio to text, sketch, or connect through your iPhone and text directly. For the last option, a notification will appear on your linked iPhone to ask if you would like to use it to text instead.

To send a message

1. Click new message on the app

2. Select the A sign beside the texting options

3. Tap the heart sign

4. Sketch with your fingers over the watch screen

5. The dot at the top right can be used to change colors

6. Click done and send.

How to use the Music App

1. Open the music app

2. At the top of the screen, tap On iPhone

3. Pick a category from your iPhone music list

4. Select your category and music and begin listening

To control the music with the device

- Tap any of the buttons, pause, or play.

- The arrow back restarts a song from scratch

- Double-tap on the back arrow to replay the previous song

- The forward arrow skips to the next song

- The Digital Crown scrolled will control the volume

Configure your mobile network

1. Set up cellular connection on your iPhone

2. Open the iPhone Apple Watch app

3. Select My Watch

4. Select Cellular

5. Select set up Cellular

6. Follow the promptings.

For family members

- Open the iPhone Apple Watch app

- Select All Watches

- Select the family members watch

- Click Done

- Select Cellular

- Select set up Cellular

- Follow the promptings.

To connect

- Go to the control center

- Turn on the connection button

How to use the Mindfulness App

To begin a reflect session

- Open the app

- Click the icon with three dots

- Select time for the session

- Select reflect and commence

- End the session by right swiping

- Then click the end button

To commence breathe session

- Open to the app and find the three dots icon

- Select breathe

- End the session by right swiping

- Then click the end button

To track and know your mindfulness rates

- Open the health app

- Search for mindfulness

- Tap on it and see the report.

To schedule mindfulness reminders

- Open the app

- Pick a day to begin and end the sessions

- You can optionally set up a custom reminder

How to use the News App
The news app is not available in all regions.

To explore stories

- Open the app

- Find the news complication and select it

- Pick a new item on Siri

- Select the news notification

To read news

- Open the app

- Use the Digital Crown to scroll stories

- Click on save for later on any story you like.

- Read it through your other compatible iPhone devices

- If you have multiple stories saved, swipe left or right to view them.

How to use the Phone call App

1. Open the app

2. Turn the Digital crown to pick a contact

3. Select the contact from your list or type a contact through the keypad

4. You can either set a facetime audio call or a normal call. The buttons are visible for both options.

5. Use the Digital Crown to control volume

Make a voice mail call

- Open the phone app

- Make a call

- At the end of an unpicked call, select voice mail

- Make your voicemail

- Send

How to use the Photos App

To copy an image

- Open the Watch app on iPhone

- Find the photos icon and select it

- Select an image to be synced

To launch the watch app

- Go to the app

- Zoom in and out with the Digital crown to see one or many images at once

How to use the Podcasts App

1. Open the app

2. Select a podcast and the episode

3. Click play

4. Explore the controls

To follow or unfollow a podcast

- Open the app

- Search for the podcast

- Select the podcast

- Select the add button to download new episodes

- Select the more button

- Select unfollow show

How to use the Reminders App

- Open the app

- Select any list

- Mark and item Done by clicking it

- Go back with the less than button

- Finished reminders are saved to a list

- To see it Select the All List

- Select the view options tab

- Select Completed

How to use the Remote App

To pair Apple watch to Apple TV

Set up your iPhone to link with the WI-Fi network of the Apple Tv

- Open the app

- Select the Apple TV

- Select Add devices

- Head to setting on the TV

- Look for remote and devices and select

- Look for remote app and devices and select

- Input the passcode on your watch

- Wait till a pairing icon appears it's done.

To control the TV

- Set the Tv to awake

- Open the app

- Select your TV

- Explore the menu using the left, right, top, and bottom swipes

- Select an item

- Use the pause and play

- Select the menu to return

- Press for long to go back to the main menu

To unpair

- Head to setting on the TV

- Look for remote and devices and select

- Look for remote apps and devices and select

- Find your apple watch

- Select unpair

- Wait till you see a lost connection icon, then you are done.

How to use the Sleep App

Open the sleep app and explore the various settings and options. You can

- Set a sleep goal

- Set sleep schedule

- Set device sleep time

- Monitor your sleep over 14 days

- Set reminders and more.

How to use the Stocks app

To add a stock

- Open the app

- Go to the end of your watch screen

- Select add stock

- Find the stock by searching

To remove a stock

- Open the app

- Find your stock list

- Tap X icon

To see details of stock

- Open the app

- Go to your stock list

- Tap on stock and explore

- Select the less than sign to return

How to use the Stopwatch App

1. Open the app

2. Select the green button to start

3. Select the red button to stop

4. Select the lap button to see the average lap time

CHAPTER TEN

Accessibility and related settings

You can explore and use the Accessibility settings.

VoiceOver

The VoiceOver allows the Apple Watch usage been without looking at the display. It works by allowing simple gestures for movement around the screen while listening as VoiceOver speaks every item you choose

Setup Watch7 using VoiceOver

1. Launch the Settings App on the Apple Watch
2. Navigate to Accessibility
3. Go to VoiceOver
4. Tao turn on VoiceOver

Utilizing VoiceOver to set up your Apple Watch

Press the digital crown three times to set it up.

Apple Watch basics with VoiceOver

You can do a host of things with the VoiceOver on your Apple Watch by swiping, pressing, and turning the digital crown.

How to use a braille display

1. Switch on a braille display
2. Navigate to Settings ok your Apple Watch
3. Accessibility, VoiceOver, braille, and select the display
4. Control your Apple Watch to see the braille commands by tapping more info

Time telling with haptic feedback

1. Launch Settings App
2. Tap Clock
3. Navigate up and tap the Taptic Time
4. Turn on Taptic Time
5. By holding two fingers on the watch face, you can. Feel haptic time version

Adjust text size and other visual settings

1. Launch the Settings App on the App Watch
2. Navigate to display and brightness
3. Go to text size
4. Use the digital crown to adjust the text to your desired size

Adjust motor skills settings

If there's trouble with using your touchscreen, adjusting the settings is possible to change how the screen responds when you touch them.

1. Launch Settings App
2. Tap motor skills
3. Explore the various settings option to fit your need.

Adjust the speed of the side key

1. Launch the Settings App on the Apple Watch
2. Navigate to Accessibility
3. Scroll to slide button click speed
4. Select the speed

How to make use of the Touch Accommodations

1. Launch the Settings app
2. Navigate to Accessibility
3. Go to touch accommodations.

4. Here, you can perform the following actions: responding to touches of a certain duration, ignoring several touches, and responding to different first or last.

Setup and use RTT

1. Launch Apple Watch on your iPhone
2. Tap "My Watch"
3. Navigate to Accessibility, then RTT
4. Turn on RTT
5. Tap relay number
6. Turn on send immediately for sending every character while typing

Make an RTT call

1. Launch the Phone app on the Apple Watch
2. Select Contacts
3. Use digital crown for scrolling

4. Tap the contacts of your choice to call
5. Scroll up
6. Tap the RTT button
7. Scribble a message

How to set the stability and mono audio parameters

1. Launch the Settings app
2. Go to accessibility, audio/ visual. You can adjust mono audio, balance, and phone noise cancellation

CHAPTER ELEVEN

Restart, reset, restore, and update

You can reset, retore, restart and update your device at any time.

How to restart WatchOS

1. Tap and hold the side button until the slider is displayed
2. Drag the Power Off to the right-hand side

How to erase WatchOS

1. Launch the Settings app
2. Navigate to General
3. Go to Reset
4. Erase all content and settings
5. Input your passcode

Restore WatchOS from a backup

Restoring Apple Watch from a backup is possible. If your watch is paired with the iPhone again,

1. Choose the restore from the backup option.

2. Select backup on your iPhone.

Update Watch software

1. Connect to Wi-Fi

2. Launch the Settings App on your Watch

3. Tap General and Scroll to Software Update

4. If there is an available update, tap to install

5. Follow instructions

CHAPTER TWELVE

Get help

Get help to handle various issues with your watch.

Sell, give away, or protect a lost Apple Watch

Ensure to unpair your Apple Watch from your iPhone if you wish to sell or give it out. This helps to remove all the information such as payment mode, activation lock. You can switch to lost mode if you misplace your Apple Watch

How to unpair your Apple Watch

1. Launch Apple Watch on your iPhone
2. Hit I next to your Watch
3. Tap unpair

1. Launch the Settings

2. Navigate to General

3. Go to About. Here, access a wide range of items.

CONCLUSION

What spoke about many things in this book, and we have finally come to an end. We hope that this book becomes very useful to you as you explore your device.

●

Made in the USA
Las Vegas, NV
25 May 2023

72503482R00075